Drawing and Learning About Horses

Using Shapes and Lines

by

Amy Bailey Muehlenhardt

Thanks to our advisers for their expertise, research, and advice:

Victor Kaneps
Co-owner of Studio Farms, Inc., Elizabeth, Colorado

Susan Kesselring, M.A., Literacy Educator
Rosemount-Apple Valley-Eagan (Minnesota) School District

Amy Bailey Muehlenhardt
grew up in Fergus Falls, Minnesota, and attended Minnesota State University in Moorhead. She holds a Bachelor of Science degree in Graphic Design and Art Education. Before coming to Picture Window Books, Amy was an elementary art teacher. She always impressed upon her students that "everyone is an artist." Amy lives in Mankato, Minnesota, with her husband, Brad.

To Craig and Brad—you both are wonderful husbands and fathers.
To my Waconia students—every time you solve a problem, you are thinking like an artist.
Be creative, and keep drawing!

ABM

Managing Editor: Bob Temple
Creative Director: Terri Foley
Editor: Sara E. Hoffmann
Editorial Adviser: Andrea Cascardi
Designer: Amy Bailey Muehlenhardt
Page production: Picture Window Books
The illustrations in this book were drawn with pencil.

Picture Window Books
5115 Excelsior Boulevard
Suite 232
Minneapolis, MN 55416
1-877-845-8392
www.picturewindowbooks.com

Printed in the United States of America.

Library of Congress Cataloging-in-Publication Data
Muehlenhardt, Amy Bailey, 1974-
Drawing and learning about horses : using shapes and lines /
by Amy Bailey Muehlenhardt
p. cm — (Sketch it!)
Summary: Provides step-by-step instructions for drawing different types of horses, using simple shapes and lines.
Includes bibliographical references.
ISBN 1-4048-0267-3 (Reinforced Library Binding)
1. Horses in art—Juvenile literature.
2. Drawing—Technique—Juvenile literature. [1. Horses in art.
2. Drawing—Technique.] I. Title.
NC783.8.H65 M84 2004
743.6'96655—dc 22

2003020000

Table of Contents

Everyone Is an Artist

There is no right or wrong way to draw!

With a little patience and some practice, anyone can learn to draw. Did you know every picture begins as a simple shape? If you can draw shapes, you can draw anything.

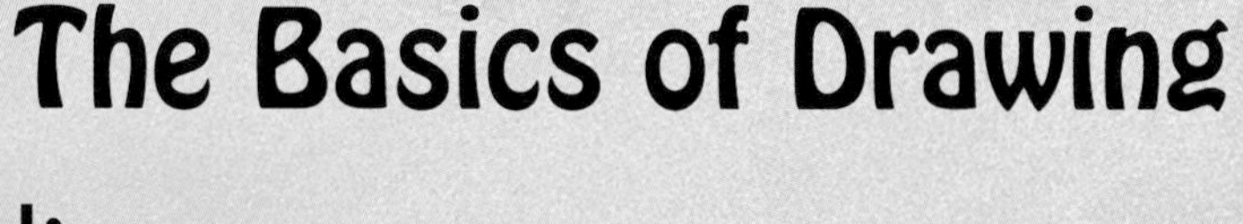

line—a long mark made by a pen, a pencil, or another tool

guideline—a line used to help you draw. The guideline will be erased when your drawing is almost complete.

shade—to color in with your pencil

value—the lightness or darkness of an object

shape—the form or outline of an object or figure

diagonal—a shape or line that leans to the side

Before you begin, you will need:

a pencil
an eraser
lots of paper

Four Tips for Drawing

1. Draw very lightly.
   To see how this is done, try drawing soft, medium, and dark lines. The softer you press, the lighter the lines will be.
2. Draw your shapes.
   Connect them with a dark, sketchy line.
3. Add details.
   Details are small things that make a good picture even better.
4. Smudge your art.
   Use your finger to rub your lines. This will soften your picture and add shadows.

Let's get started!

Simple shapes help you draw.

Practice drawing these shapes before you begin:

circle

A circle is round like a bouncing ball.

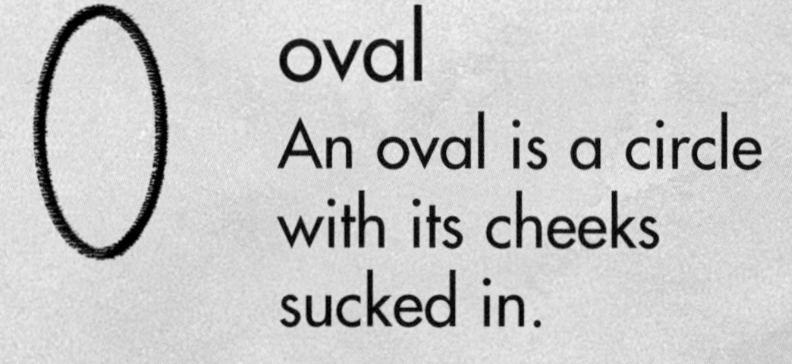

oval

An oval is a circle with its cheeks sucked in.

arc

An arc is half of a circle. It looks like a turtle's shell.

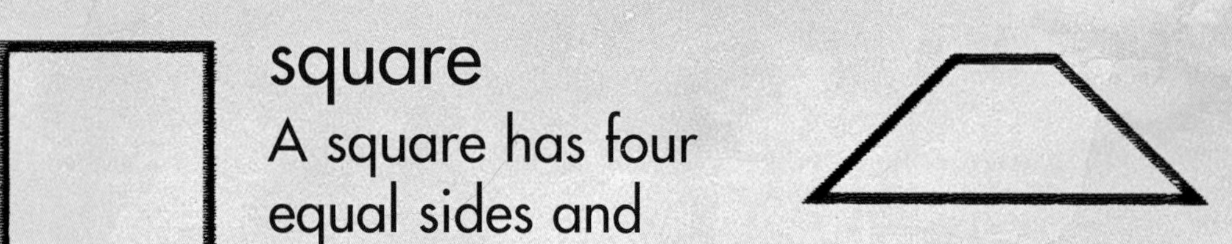

square

A square has four equal sides and four corners.

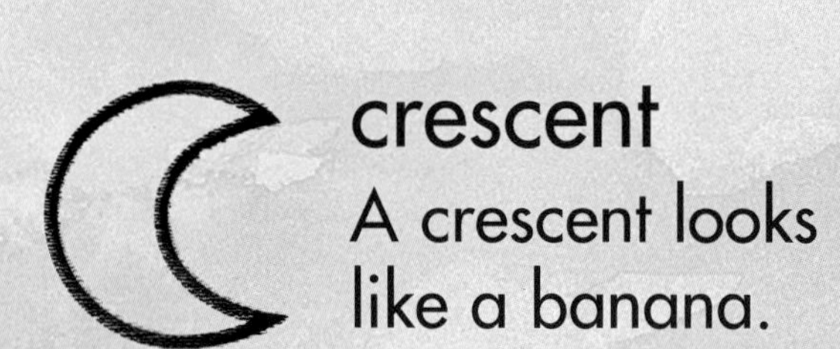

crescent

A crescent looks like a banana.

triangle

A triangle has three sides and three corners.

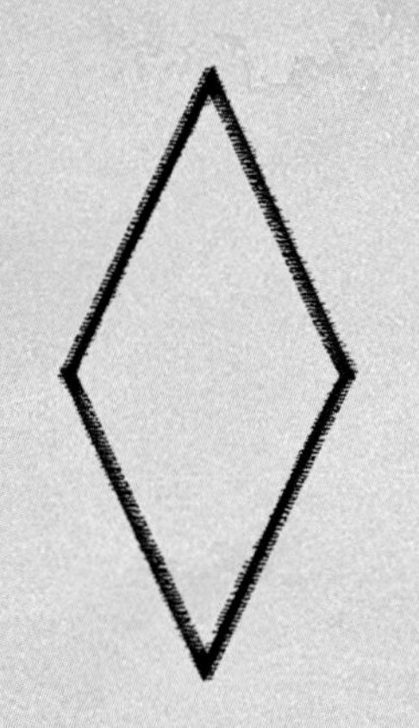

diamond

A diamond is two triangles put together.

trapezoid

A trapezoid has four sides and four corners. Two of its sides are different lengths.

rectangle

A rectangle has two long sides, two short sides, and four corners.

You will also use lines when drawing.

Practice drawing these lines:

vertical

A vertical line stands tall like a tree.

horizontal

A horizontal line lies down and takes a nap.

diagonal

A diagonal line leans to the side.

dizzy

A dizzy line spins around and around.

zig zag

A zig-zag line is sharp and pointy.

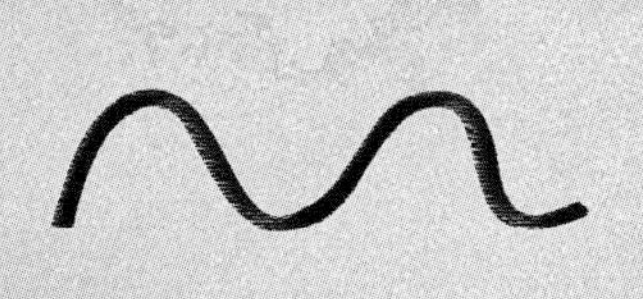

wavy

A wavy line moves up and down like a roller coaster.

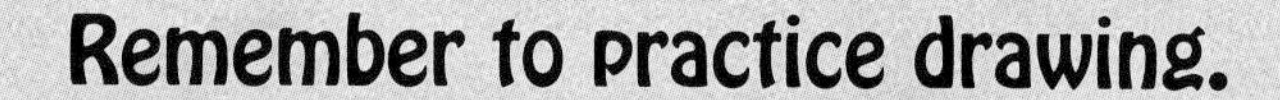

Remember to practice drawing.

While using this book, you may want to stop drawing at step five or six. That's great! Everyone is at a different drawing level.

Don't worry if your picture isn't perfect. The important thing is to have fun. You may wish to add details to your drawing. Is your horse near a barn? Is it in a field? Create a background.

Be creative!

Quarter Horse

Quarter horses have powerful muscles, small ears, and large eyes. Their backs are wide and sloping. Quarter horses are used for barrel racing, cargo carrying, and to tend and herd cattle. They come in 13 solid colors.

Step 1

Draw an oval for the head and a circle for the muzzle.

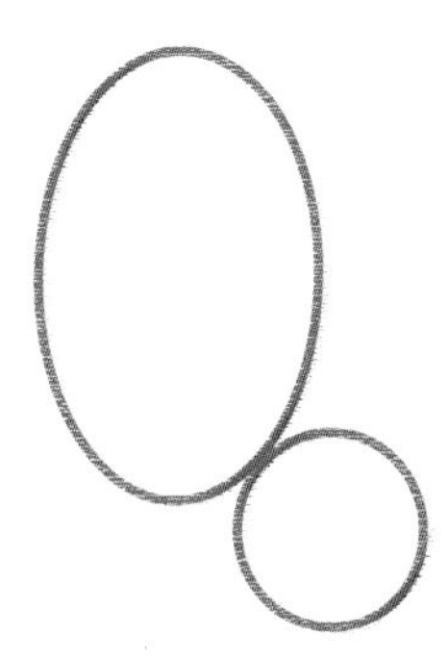

Step 2

Connect the head and the muzzle with two curved lines. Add two arcs for the eyes.

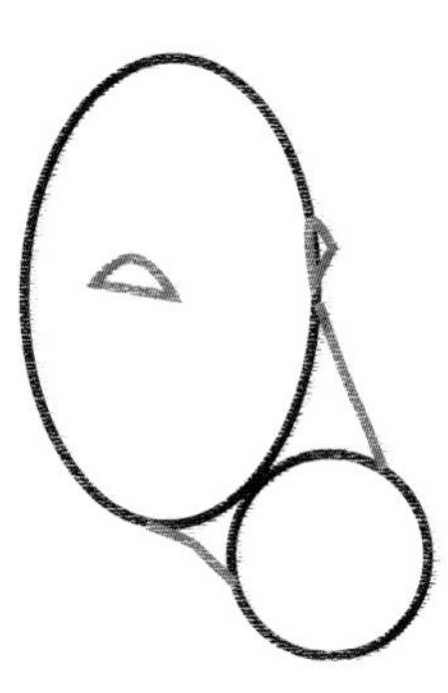

Step 3

Draw two long curving lines for the neck. Add a circle for the nostril and a diagonal line for the mouth.

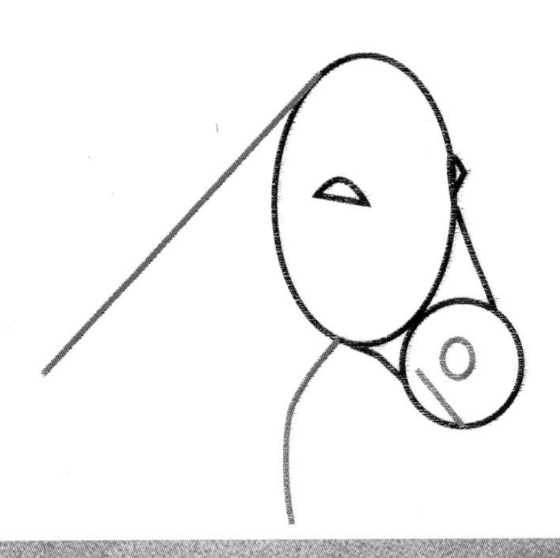

Step 4

Draw two triangles for ears. Add a circle and two curving lines along the face and below the ear for the bridle.

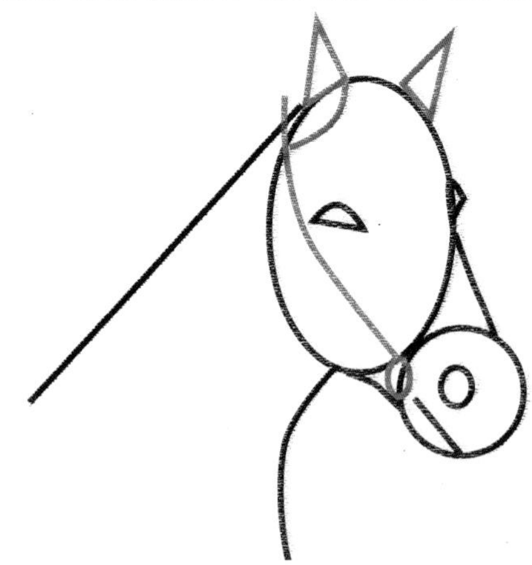

Step 5

Add short, wavy lines for the mane. Add two curved lines and two circles for the reigns.

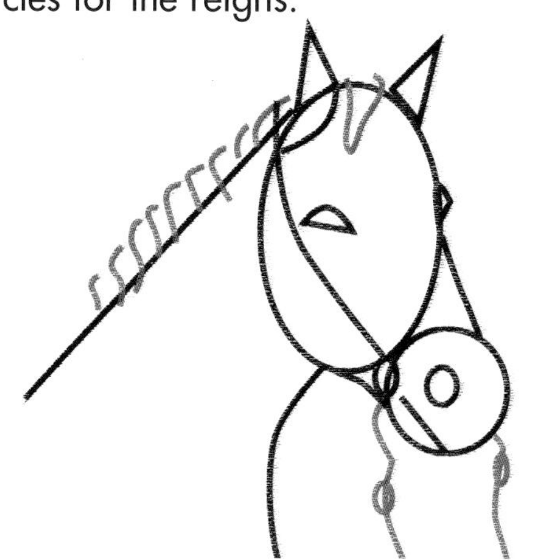

Step 6

Connect the shapes with a darker, sketchy line. Draw a wavy heart for the marking on the forehead. Begin shading the horse.

Step 7

Shade in the horse using the side of your pencil. Leave the heart marking white. Darken the eye, nostril, and ears.

Canadian Horse and Filly

Canadian horses were originally bred in France. They are known as the "little iron horses" because they are sturdy. Canadian horses are very rare. At one time, these horses were nearly extinct.

Step 1

Draw an oval for the horse's body. Draw a circle at each end of the oval. Draw a smaller oval for the filly. Draw a circle at each end of the oval.

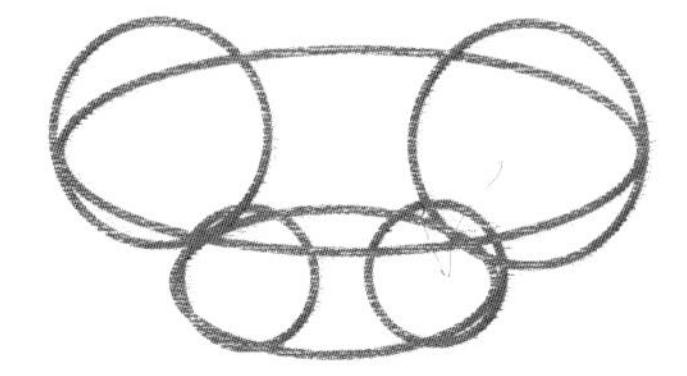

Step 2

Draw two circles for the heads. Draw two smaller circles for the muzzles. On both the horse and filly, connect the head and muzzle with two short lines. Draw two curving lines for the horse's neck.

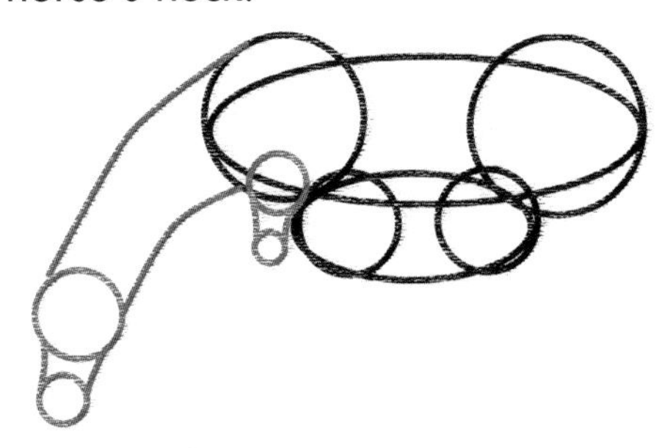

Step 3

Draw seven ovals for the horse's and filly's upper thighs. Draw seven circles for the knees. One of the horse's thighs is hidden.

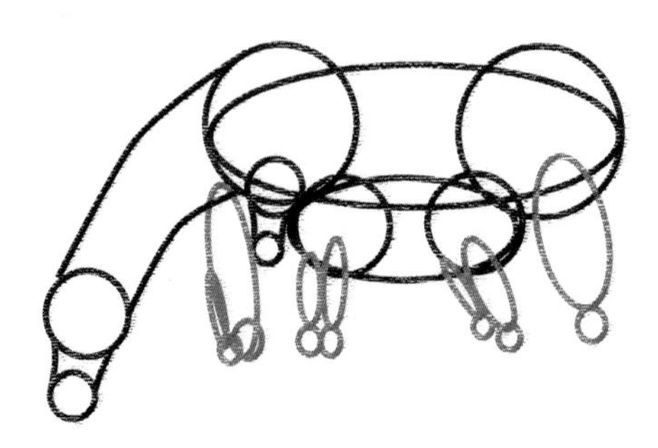

Step 4

Draw eight rectangles for the shins. Add eight trapezoids for the hooves.

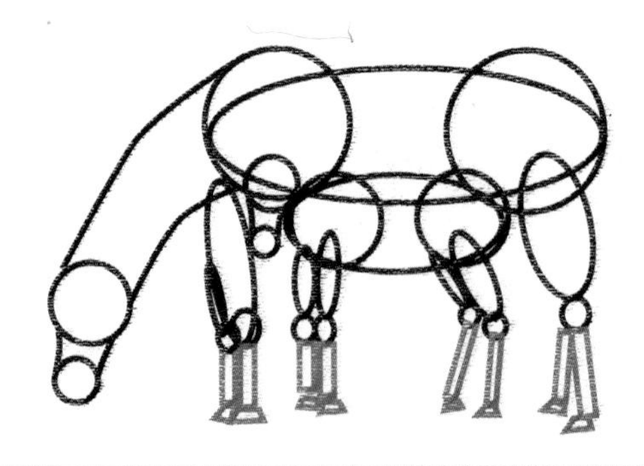

Step 5

Draw an arc for the horse's eye. Add an oval for the nostril. Draw two arcs for the filly's eyes. Add two ovals for the nostrils. Draw four triangles for ears. Add curved lines for the manes and tails.

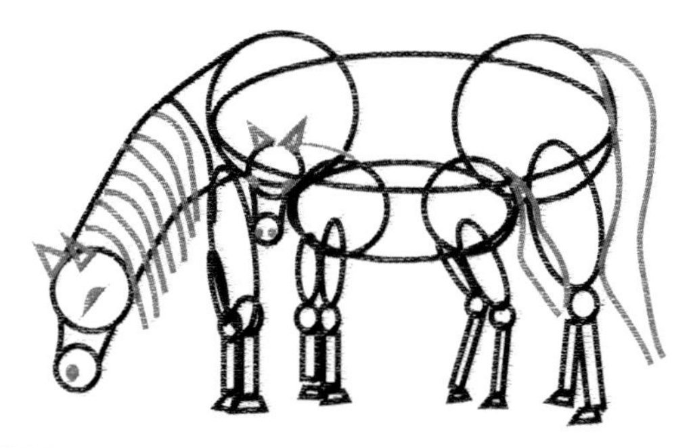

Step 6

Connect the shapes with a darker, sketchy line. Watch how the two circles are connected to create the horse's back. Begin erasing the shapes inside. Add two curved lines for the marking on the filly's head.

Step 7

Continue erasing the inside shapes. Shade in the horse and filly using the side of your pencil. Leave the marking on the filly's head white. Shade in the manes, tails, eyes, and nostrils.

Clydesdale

Clydesdales are very large horses with gentle personalities. They have well-defined markings on their faces. Clydesdales have four white socks, or bands, on their shins. They are usually brown, or brown with black manes and tails.

Step 1

Draw an oval for the body. Draw a big circle on each end of the oval.

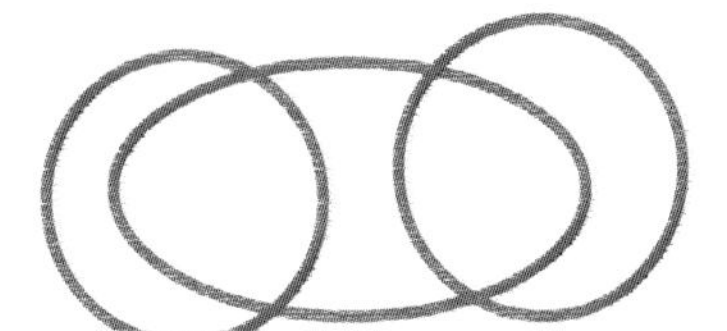

Step 2

Draw a circle for the head and a smaller circle for the muzzle. Connect the head and muzzle with two short lines. Draw two curving lines for the neck.

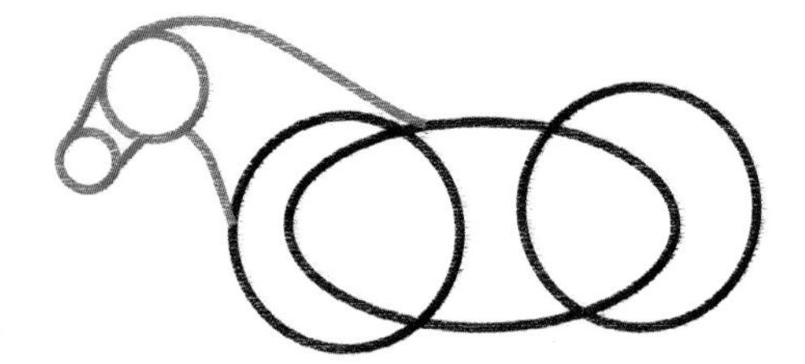

Step 3

Draw four ovals for the thighs. Add four circles for the knees.

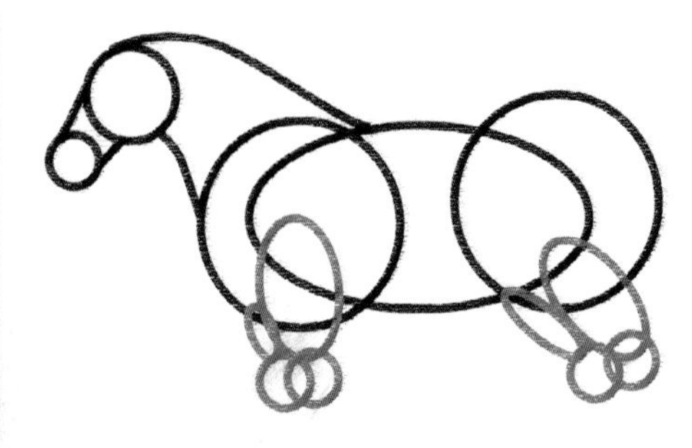

Step 4

Below the knees, add large trapezoids for the long hair on the horse's hooves. Add short lines for the mane.

Step 5

Draw two triangles for ears. Draw an arc for the eye and an oval for the nostril. Draw several ovals for the mane and a larger oval for the tail sprig decoration.

Step 6

Connect the shapes with a darker, sketchy line. Begin erasing the shapes inside. Add a diagonal line for the mouth. Draw a curved line for the marking on the horse's head.

Step 7

Shade in the horse using the side of your pencil. Add a short line inside the ovals for the mane decoration. Leave the hair on the hooves white.

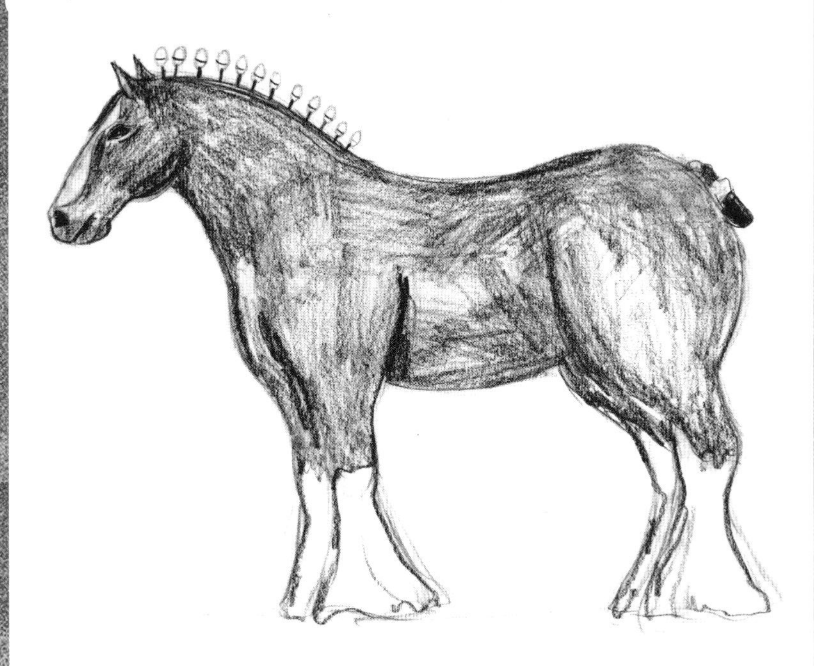

Palomino Horse

Palominos have white manes, white tails, and golden coats. Horses of many different breeds can be palominos. Palominos are used for ranching, riding, rodeos, and parades.

Step 1

Draw a circle for the head. Draw a small circle for the muzzle.

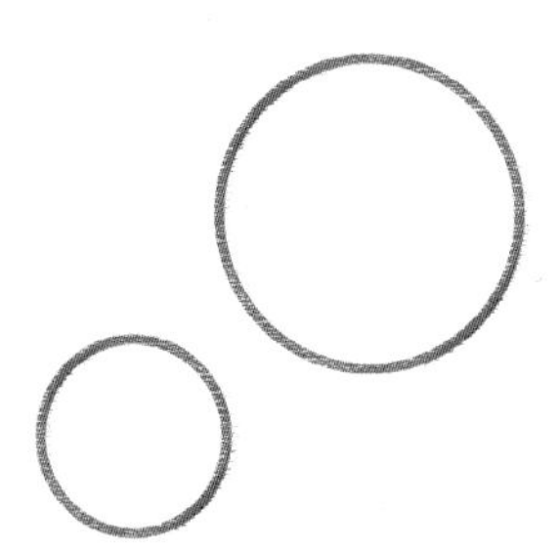

Step 2

Connect the head and the muzzle with two curving lines.

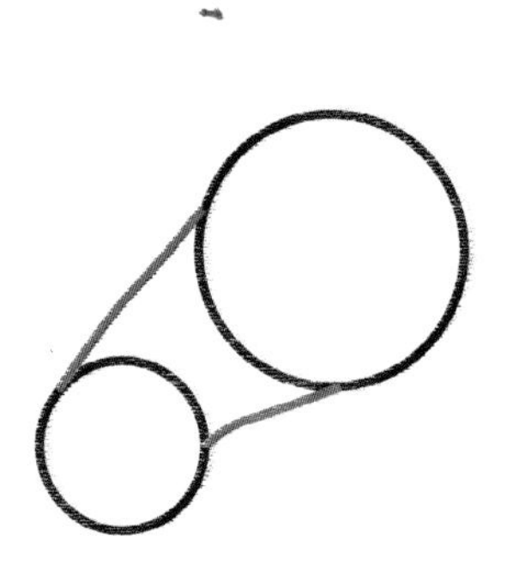

Step 3

Draw two curving lines for the neck.

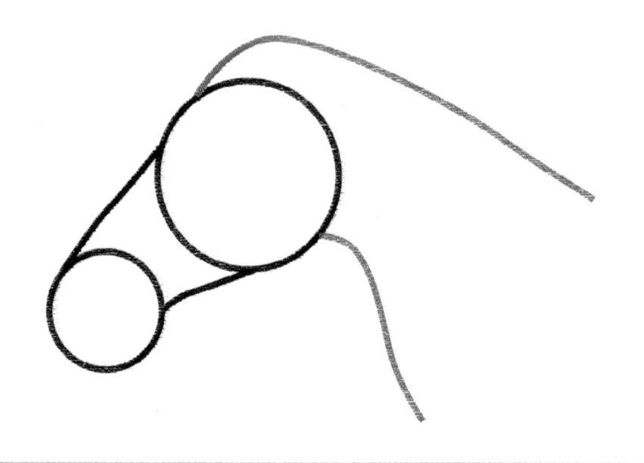

Step 4

Draw an arc for the eye. Add a small circle inside the arc for the pupil. Draw a circle for the nostril. Draw a diagonal line for the mouth.

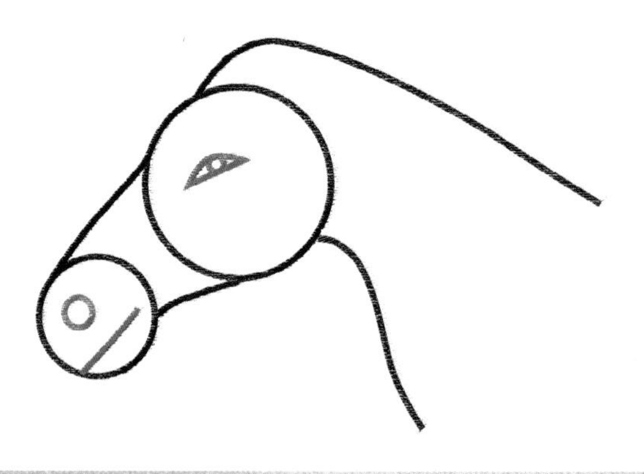

Step 5

Draw two triangles for the ears. Add two zig-zag lines for the mane.

Step 6

Connect the shapes with a darker, sketchy line. Begin erasing the shapes inside. Add curved lines around the eye. Begin shading.

Step 7

Continue shading in the horse. Darken the eye and nostril. Leave the mane white.

Pinto

Pintos were brought to North America by Spanish explorers. They have two color patterns: white with large, colored spots, or dark with white spots. *Pinto* means *painted* in Spanish.

Step 1

Draw a diagonal oval for the body. Add a circle at each end of the oval. Draw a circle for the head. Draw a small circle for the muzzle.

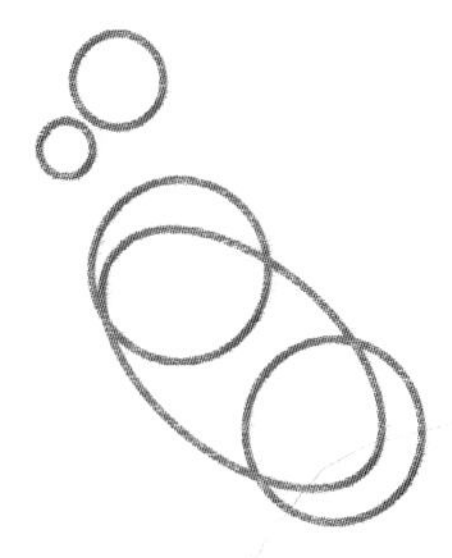

Step 2

Connect the muzzle, head, and body with three curving lines. Add an arc for the eye. Draw three ovals for the thighs. The fourth leg is hidden.

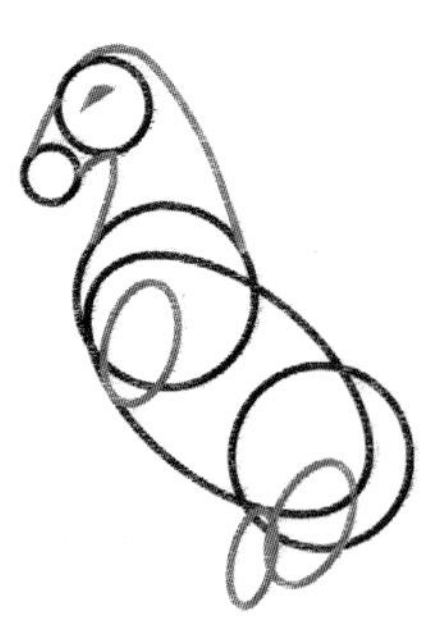

Step 3

Draw a circle for the nostril and a diagonal line for the mouth. Draw three rectangles, three circles, and three rectangles for the legs.

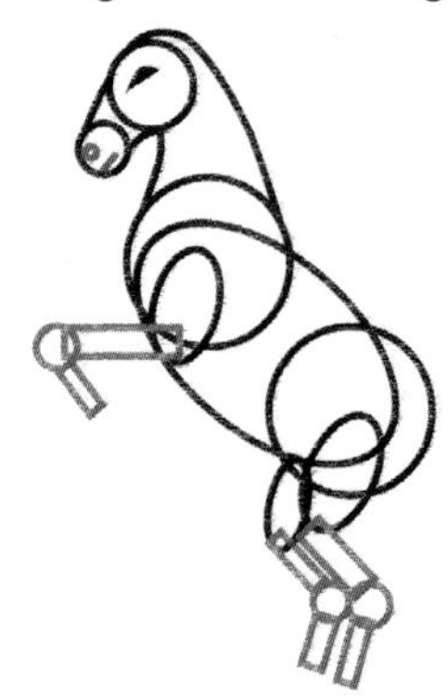

Step 4

Draw three circles at the bottoms of the rectangles. Draw three trapezoids for the hooves. Draw two triangles for ears.

Step 5

On the far side, draw a rectangle for the leg. Add a circle knee and a small rectangle for the shin. Add curved lines for the mane and tail.

Step 6

Connect the shapes with a darker, sketchy line. Begin erasing the shapes inside. Add curved lines for the pinto's spots. Shade in the mane and tail.

Step 7

Continue adding curved lines to the mane and tail. Shade in the pinto's spots. Leave some areas white. Shade in the nostril, eye, and hooves.

Thoroughbred

Thoroughbreds have full chests and long, straight legs. They are very tall. Thoroughbreds are used for track racing, jumping, and pleasure riding. They eat corn, oats, bran, and carrots. Thoroughbreds come in solid colors, such as black and chestnut.

Step 1

Draw a long oval for the body. Draw a circle at each end of the oval. Draw a circle for the head and a smaller circle for the muzzle.

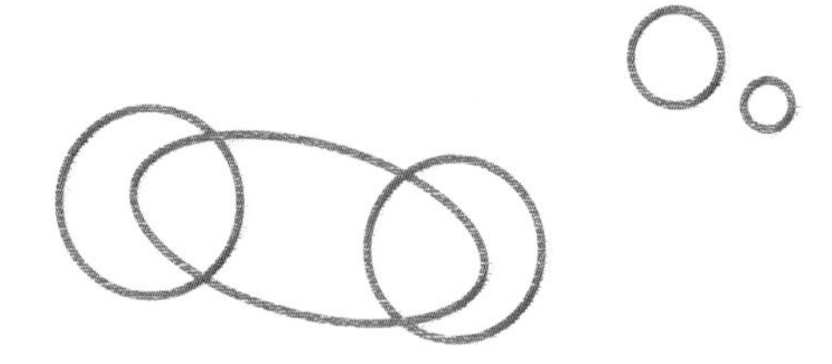

Step 2

Connect the muzzle, head, and body with four curving lines. Draw an oval and a circle for the jockey. Add a circle for the horse's thigh.

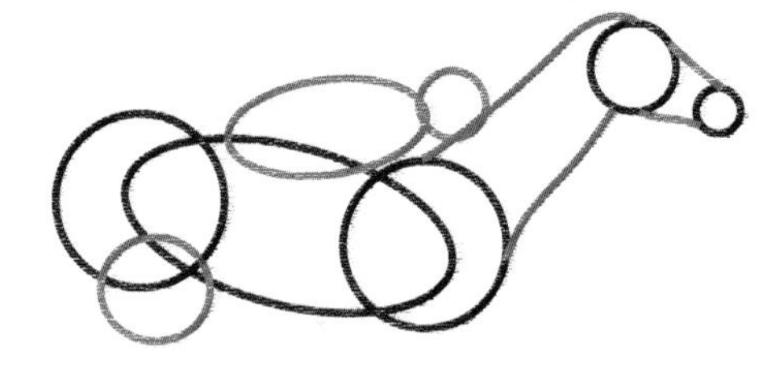

Step 3

Draw three ovals for the jockey's arm and leg. Draw four rectangles for the horse's legs. Add four circles for the knees.

Step 4

Draw an arc for the jockey's hat. Draw four rectangles and four circles for the horse's legs. Add two triangles for ears. Draw an arc and an oval for the eye and the nostril.

Step 5

Draw four trapezoids for the hooves. Draw curved lines for the mane and the tail. Add a circle for the jockey's hand. Draw a rectangle and an oval for the boot.

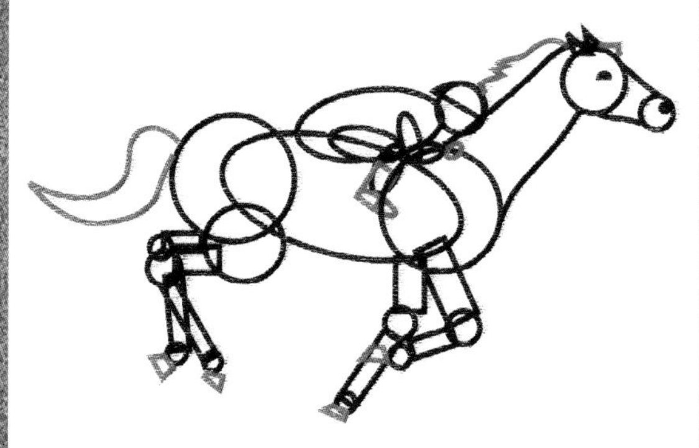

Step 6

Connect the shapes with a darker, sketchy line. Begin erasing the shapes inside. Add a small circle and lines for the bridle and reigns.

Step 7

Shade in the horse with the side of your pencil. Darken the mane, tail, eye, and nostril. Shade in the jockey's boot, shirt, and pants.

Shetland Pony

Shetland ponies are very small. They have strong hind legs and long heads. Shetlands have very full manes and tails. They were used as workhorses in the mines of England and Scotland. Shetland ponies are good with children. They are very gentle.

Step 1

Draw an oval for the body. Draw a circle at each end of the oval. The back circle should be larger. Draw a circle for the head and a smaller circle for the muzzle.

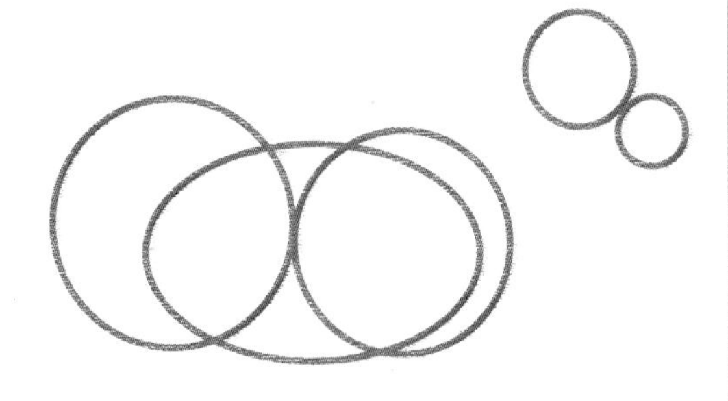

Step 2

Connect the muzzle, head, and body with four curving lines. Add four ovals for the thighs.

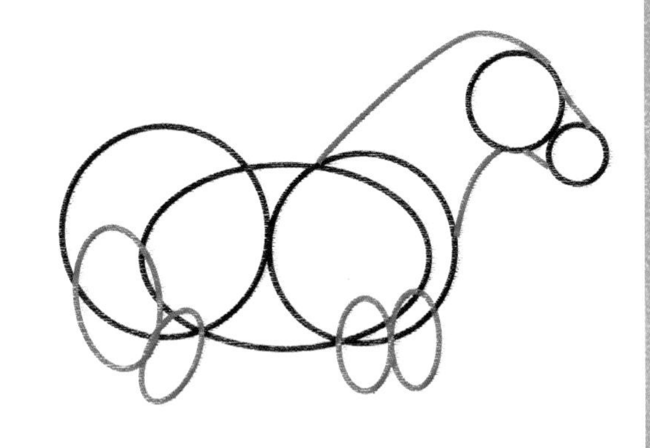

Step 3

Draw four circles for the knees. Add four squares for the legs. Draw a triangle for the eye.

Step 4

Draw four circles for the joints. Add four trapezoids for the hooves. Draw a circle for the nostril.

Step 5

Draw two triangles for ears. Draw curved lines for the long mane and tail.

Step 6

Connect the shapes with a darker, sketchy line. Begin erasing the shapes inside.

Step 7

Continue erasing the lines you no longer need. Shade in using the side of your pencil. Darken the hair, eye, and nostril.

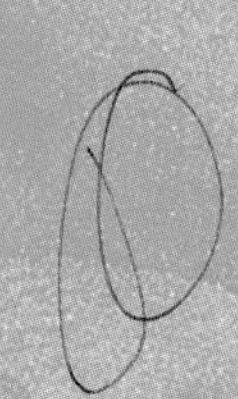

Arabian Filly

Arabians have large nostrils, small ears, and long, flowing manes and tails. Arabians are used in competitions, trail riding, racing, and pleasure riding. They eat hay, grasses, oats, and bran.

Step 1

Draw an oval for the body. Draw a circle at each end of the oval. Draw a circle for the head. Add a smaller circle for the muzzle.

Step 2

Connect the head and the muzzle with two diagonal lines. Draw a large oval and a rectangle for the thigh. Draw a smaller oval and rectangle for the front leg.

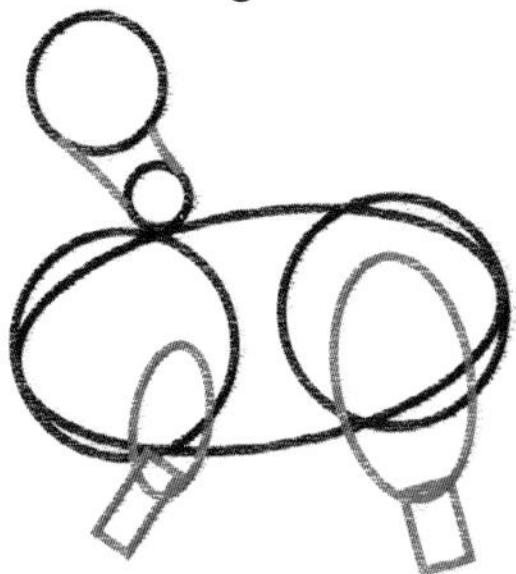

Step 3

Connect the head and the chest with two curved lines for the neck. Draw two circles for the knees. Add two rectangles for the lower legs.

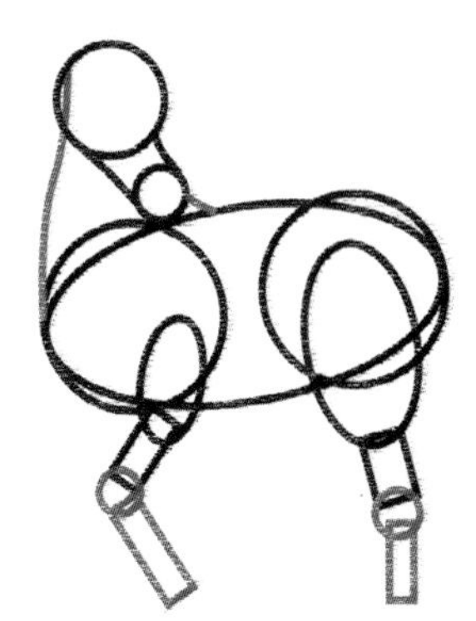

Step 4

On the far side, draw two ovals for the thighs. Draw two rectangles for the thigh and lower leg. Add a crescent tail.

Step 5

Draw four trapezoids for the hooves. Add two arcs for eyes and two ovals for nostrils. Draw two triangles for the ears.

Step 6

Connect your shapes with a darker, sketchy line. Begin erasing the shapes inside. Add curved lines around the eyes. Draw curved lines for hair.

Step 7

Continue erasing your shapes. Shade in using the side of your pencil. Darken the tail, mane, eyes, and nostrils.

To Learn More

At the Library

Ames, Lee J. *Draw 50 Horses*. Garden City, N.Y.: Doubleday, 1984.

Emberley, Ed. *Ed Emberley's Drawing Book of Animals*. Boston: Little, Brown & Co., 1994.

Hammond, Lee. *Draw Horses*. Cincinnati, Ohio: North Light Books, 2001.

Randolph, Joanne. *Let's Draw a Horse With Rectangles*. New York: PowerKids Press, 2004.

Stewart, Gail B. *The Arabian Horse*. Mankato, Minn.: Capstone Press, 1995

On the Web

Fact Hound

Fact Hound offers a safe, fun way to find Web sites related to this book. All of the sites on Fact Hound have been researched by our staff.
http://www.facthound.com

1. Visit the Fact Hound home page.
2. Enter a search word related to this book, or type in this special code:1404802673.
3. Click on the FETCH IT button.

Your trusty Fact Hound will fetch the best sites for you!